Even the Weapons

poems

by M. D. Dunn

BuschekBooks

Ottawa

Library and Archives Canada Cataloguing in Publication

Dunn, Mark D., 1969-, author
    Even the weapons : poems / by M.D. Dunn.

ISBN 978-1-894543-83-5 (pbk.)

    I. Title.

PS8557.U548517E84 2014   C811'.6   C2014-907315-1

Cover Image: Cover Image by Maria Parrella-Ilaria, B&W photograph,
altered

Printed in Winnipeg, Manitoba, Canada by Hignell Book Printing.

BuschekBooks
P.O. Box 74053
5 Beechwood Avenue
Ottawa, Ontario, Canada K1M 2H9
www.buschekbooks.com

This one's for Kim,

and for Maria

Table of Contents

In Human Rhythms

First Poems

Find the road.
It runs through the hearts of
everyone you love.

It is by chance
that you found the road.

When you lose the road,
it is the beginning of absence
and the high branch of loneliness
reaching from your depth,

to know the whole face of you,
to rest in the crook of song
hinged in your throat
before the words go out,

leaving stars and smoke and

—We live in sad houses
with joy all around.

Crimes

At dinner, I said we lit the lampless night
with butane from a squeeze can,
drew pentagrams and hard words
on asphalt down the wooded lane.

When the hill went orange with headlights,
we dropped the match and hid
to watch the cars swerve or brake,
speed up and speed away—

but to write that poem is galdor-craft
I am not willing to make, can't imagine
the years to do it. What gods in fields
would loan their tongues?

Do you believe it is a crime
to write about the gods?
Go on, scatter your denial.

For green I am in darkness,
pretending to laugh at the fear I've released,

and missing the night without fire.

Sustaining Wonder

The priest's slate face showed the wine
to be wine and the body flatbread.

Unless bored with miracles,
he'd raise a brow
to the punk taste of blood.

Unless accustomed to blood.

The lime suit made me itch,
and that itch became Sunday.
My mother in the pew, the only one sitting
with us marching for the wafer.

I imagined she looked sad,
her head bowed in the appearance of prayer.
She was the only one who never mentioned God.

And I was never old enough for the wine.
Then, once of age, uninterested.
But I wobbled in line for my disc of flesh.
The feel of it, like a tin slug.
And beneath the choir,
the sound of it in my hand,
the slow rush of callused feet
across sand, caught
like a note never sung.

Night Walk

Is to stand on water
as to bang my head?

I too
fly the moon
with the moon
in its season.

What else are dreams for
but to crawl in the low brush;
what else is the earth for
but to hold your dreams
in place while you sleep?

Whitefish Island, May

Secret is
there are no
secrets. Everything is
what it seems.

Old gods in this place
know that I'm here.

I pass by, tolerated.

You, too, could pass by

a scene at the water's edge—

the bare cross on its hill, a song
charged with aggressing violins,
a dashboard Christ,
its spring head on the curb—

and see only concrete and concrete.

The Line

Then the line was no line.
Was I the man in the wheel chair
climbing the ramp from low water,
the marina's hulls and sails between us,

hearing his lungs,
his tendons singing
almost the slip and grind
of his sockets?

Of this moment: I am in a park
not far from the water,
swatting flies from my legs
and writing this down.

At the top of the ramp
a woman and a child
look to the river,
to the slow curl of day advancing

and say nothing,
and do not want to.

Eventually

The living rings of distant giants
are measured in human rhythms.

Blue comet, red at the tail,
is faster than the star it worships,
and unfixed for us.

The sky must set its memory
in dawn and dusk, the actions
of beings desperate for time.

You may be lost for a while,
with eyes for dawn when it moves
like a god through the night.

Have patience. Even the weapons
are tired of fighting.

The Power of Song

on mother's knee,
we sang the School Days song
that ends with you riding my sleigh.

The Fifth Horseman, Browsing

He is late with his gift of memory.
Devastation, everything in wastelands,
or will be in wastelands—
depending.

And we like the Fifth Horseman,
or liked him—again, depending—
because he brings nostalgia,
and who doesn't like nostalgia?
Images to pine for and moon over.

It can never last. Before long
the Fifth Horseman's a scar
and the beauty he carries a murmur
that threatens my retirement fund
and spoils a promising dinner.

Prophecy and history, he says,
are determined by what has happened,
or what will happen and whether
that or this has influence.

One Summer

Strings from the lake
when the sun
draws the next
day's rain
is how
my mother
said clouds were made.

She sat in the chair
with its legs
in the lawn,
with yellow florets
all around,
beginning to laugh.

Yesterday

The crows and their manic dance
while I walk through snow
with scraps from last night's meal.

January Thaw

Chickadees in the morning
drink from pools on the deck.
Rain from a clear sky.
In her housecoat and sandals,
she is out at dawn with her camera.

Men on the lake last week
died and the paper has them pictured
with a clothesline of fish
strung between them.
Today the channel is clear.

Remembrance Day

i.

But that was last night.
Early in the morning, maybe,
and it's snowed for hours,
heavy like the first snowfall,
and I am sitting in the courtesy lounge
at the dealership garage.
The television is a box of prehistory
irradiating the plastic room, my walk-in closet
with eight chairs, garbage can, and table
coughing its magazines to the floor.

There are three of us waiting:
one woman is sending her mind
with her thumbs into minds far away;
and a man like an outlaw in the corner,
white ropes from his ears to a box.
He calls someone, speaks like he is
alone in the room; without shame,
he says his name is Mark.

The television now: The Prime Minister
just before his holiday
enters the mass, the band plays
O Canada. "There will be no commentary,"
the announcer says.

ii.

A cellphone bleats with the ring of a sheep
and her thumbs begin. The showroom is murder
with pitch and pinch, a sale and loss,
accusations, and the television
broadcasting its silence beneath their faces,
the oldest living soldiers.
Cannon fire begins and ends
in silence, a moment's peace
in the pockets of war.

I run in out of space, weight
dragging on too much self.
Summer holds the door
open for winter to pass.

We practice for war
and pray to war
and take our war
anywhere we find it.

The cannon's shout is prayer,
robes wounded with poppies.
We have become an I-am-not-
self-recognizable blip of light.

More bleating. The man named Mark
is called away.

In last night's dream the shovel
scraped the back step.

I dipped the blade into a puddle
that once had night on its face,
buried the blade in earth
like a gift to the Earth.

Wash it away. Wash it away.
New winter, let me speak.

iii.

And boom! I am back to the place I forget.
In the lighting section at the Canadian Tire,
proving I exist when the bulbs snap
on as I pass down the aisle.

The merfolk of Europa
are not thrilled with the drills
and buckets, the broadcasts
of chainsaws, the canned
slaughter of forests we are
about to send.

I broadcast you, your rare science,
and dream it was just like this:

in the lighting section
of the sky's broad lens.

You'd think me a bird,
and you might not be wrong.

Think me into something.
If you leave me unthought,
who will stand for Europa?

Two Postcards

1. I have found my ditch at last—
   it's a walk from the stop
   where I stood for the bus,
   not far from the oil tanks.
   It is morning. I have not yet arrived.

2. Tuesday, and a man doesn't play the piano
   in the dancehall near the dining lounge
   where we struggle with soup and Thursday.
   No one has noticed
   I've not dreamt in a week.

A Most Inaccurate History of Contemplation

Mastering the koan,
rap in tight puzzlement
to stall the new radicalism
that threatens free-market verse
in the latter-half of late
middle age, and thereby
set the standard for confusion.

One Master says,
Folk music in ordinary keys
is heinous unless played
with imaginary instruments.

Another Master will find
there is nothing ordinary
about anything and nothing.

Listening, pretend to remember
the original tune, pretend
to tap your feet, to applaud
on the way to the door.

Tiger moths remember Alexandria
when library windows are open.

The Ages Of

Copycat

Immigrant kid with exotic bread:
dark rye and pumpernickel.
Words our fathers drank or never said.

The boy with the buffalo tongue sandwich
and the last name mocked in rhyme.
Baby teeth and murder on our breath.

This was the slow hell of childhood,
and this the new hell now:

loneliness through clicks and keys;
drugs designed for early sleep;
everyone with dust around their feet.

While all that we have learned to forget
pry long fingers into what is seen
and what we never talk about.

The boy who hanged himself
was said to have slipped
or fallen asleep while forgetting
rid himself of pain altogether.

And from that day
our minds made nothing
but doors and nooses.

Old Garden River

The river and its roots in him.
His depth as deep as clay.

He stayed hours on the stone
until there was nothing left
between his mind and the river.

Each thought in a leaf
twisting untouched,
obsessive in a spiral
pool near the matted branches
of a fallen birch.

That river leading to branches,
built from the branches above it,
feeding the system of rivers
you could follow to the channel,

and David walking the banks.
Each bend was a helix homing down,
a root to its seed.

Walking only so far
to keep the myth
of the lake at the end.

Woodlot

In winter the timber has fallen.
White flashes grey with fox
and rabbit play, summer's tree
bare as a cross, a white pine
with its needle crown around it
in the snow.

Watch then for wolves.
Good neighbour Pinter said he'd come back
and tracked away loaded with wood.

He'd be back like he said,
but why leave David in the woods alone?

He wore the stillness like a hand,
crows in the branches above him.

It must have been a gift
that Pinter left the boy.
He'd learn his stillness from the stillness
in winter.

Trees in their stretch to the sun
open like canvas can open
with the movement of a brush.
It is posture we admire in trees,
in art.

The boy learned silence
in the whole silence of winter.
How a twig under the weight of snow
will sound for miles.

Now a nuthatch on the pine bark
miles away through quiet
and right behind, wolves.
He saw them at the bus stop
in the morning, waiting.

Eyes in the white fur
stopped in the lane, measuring.

A chill not from the cold,
the soul cringing at the steady eyes—
memories from the time before names,
before the division of you from me.
That is where the wolf will live.
From there,
chill the soul
know the noise from the kill,
the blood in the snow,
the long strides after—

A Reminder

We have lived
longer under stars
than under street lights.

It is obvious,
but it needed
to be said.

The Ages of

i.

He is pulling the roots out of loam.
The tree he is climbing is the same
tree he destroyed.

On the sliding hill, the house below,
the lithe forest—its rivers hidden—
sprawling before him,

David, the sky opening in voice,
the man in the car stopping roadside,
"It will all come down

On you one day. It will come down."
He had not destroyed anything yet,
but shuddered with guilt.

ii.

He was born in time to mourn the woods.
Born to profit from the destruction,
in time for the loss.

The worm that ate grandfather's forest
goes east and bifurcates at Wharncliffe:
one limb south, one north.

The south arm brings electricity
to cities and towns that matter:
Toronto et al;

the north arm barely humming with wires.
A few strands to James Bay and beyond.
David didn't know.

It was easy to claim ignorance,
but he heard death in the constant whine:
machines eat the ground.

iii.

And money was not easily found.
David's first job was pulling out sticks
that once were his trees.

His father hoped he'd learn about work,
the value of money and savings,
how the buck is earned.

He learned all that, but more, he observed
that beauty is at odds with progress,
and progress must end.

"What else could have been done with the land?"
the old man, years after it was gone.
It could not just be.

Along the worm trail through the forest
men built metal towers, skeletons
for electric wires.

iv.

In his last years Grampa remembered
the rise, fall, each civilization
revealing itself

in colour foldouts of magazines,
in the way trees sighed in winter
and laughed through summer.

He felt the aches of his body as
tremors that freed him from history,
stones and layered sand,

and still we arose and were aware,
for a short time played at dance and struggle.
Just like anyone.

v.

From satellite, it is a silt patch
stretching fingers toward the wood lots
and yards of houses.

The worm eats green, cores out the centre.
The worm eats hope, feeds on the spirit.
Everything good is gone.

Put him outside everything he loved.
Put him in chains, open to the sky.
Everything good is gone.

"It will all come down on you one day."
He thought of this when the tractor died.
Sugar in its tank.

There had been warnings, patterns scattered
in drained cups, rain-washed notes pinned
to the green shed's door.

Sprayed in gold paint the word "Ecocide"
on the bucket of the payloader.
But what did it mean?

What else could have been done with the land?
The trees had stood and the trees were gone.
He had no power.

All summer he wrenched the dark earth,
pulled out sticks and rocks for five dollars an hour
and dreamed of leaving.

The world might die around us and we,
obsessed with mazes, watch with no thought
until nothing's left.

Tornados announced with sepia light,
the sky gone jaundice before the storm.
He brought in his toys.

The Ages of, Fragmentary

one house with brown siding
at the bottom of the sliding hill
the woods nearby

a slow fall that leads to the river
where everything is born to begin
where everything mounts

in colour before the white descent
all red all fire before the winter
all sweet and sleepless

David dreamt escape, stood vigils
at windows, the seasons' rotation
counted in decades

He wanted to stay in the autumn,
to stay the wintry press.

Tried to see with Blake's infinite eye
the forest, the river and clay banks
where our minds were invented
from rusted ploughs, abandoned,
and the fields all wild,
the river before its chains.

A late winter with tornadoes.
This summer, the forests will burn.

So the earth knows its boundary
by the spaces we leave.

There is no fire that does not burn.
Something is consumed in exchange for light

Later he bought land
but would not sell a tree from it.

The sticks he pulled from the soil
were the trees he'd climbed
and sat beneath. He saw faeries
in bushes, and spoke
voiceless with beings in the gorge.

In good years, the rings are far apart
with space between each line.

From age three to age nine he never
thought about it and the forest
settled around him.

Creatures of the sky and light:

Woodpecker hammers
an aluminium pole
because there is reward in ritual.

By May, grackles have chased the crows away.

I am losing my garden to last year's canopy.

He made stories from broken things.
The carpet of green, broken.
The bits of trees, all that was left.

A belief in redemption,
sin and forgiveness
kept him from transformation.

It comes around, seed to stalk,
tree to mulch. It comes around
with no guidance or prompting,
only the faintest participation,
watching, nothing more.
Observation is our contribution.

Boy in the Grass

And this is where he lived.
Here he watched seasons,
waited for the ice to open
a channel in the ocean
he could not see
from his land-locked home.

The owls knew the direction he'd take.
Late in the tramped field—
the game over, everyone exhausted—
they watched stars in the dense night.
A few shooting by, sparking out.
Others in their slow arcs, committed.

When there was nothing to read
or watch, people read the stars.
He knew of astrology, knew his sign,
the signs of those he loved,
but could not find their bodies
etched in the swirl above him.

One teacher said looking into night
was looking back through time,
but time had yet to occur to him.
There was no time where he lived.
Only the damp grass under his hands,
a bat in its falling flight, or an owl passing.

Somewhere he'd learned that owls meant death.
The silence of the jagged bird,
hard eyes against the night,
a character trespassing from dream.
Head turning as it passed, soundless to the woods.

In the morning he walked to the river down back.
The clay banks three times his height.
The wake once so high to eat the field,
now a trickling sound from the lake
in the hills through a pathless forest.

David's Geography of Regret

This is where he should have kissed you:
the ring of pines he can never walk through.

So where can they go
but Horton's on a Tuesday?
Swamped air and industry
hanging in the heat.

To sit on concrete,
with the lawn nearby.
The green's a place
for cigarettes,
a place to spit.

Their laughter folds around itself
before dropping underfoot.

Postscript

There is a Japanese word
for unwanted favours
that cause more problems
than they solve.

A situation that English
might describe as
"Thanks for nothing."

Walking the Grounds of the Old House

Bucket by bucket, he dug out the hillside,
braced the beams with logs on jacks,
padded walls with stone—long before me.

I remember the whitewashed logs
that ran the length of the ceiling,
the workbench and the grinding wheel
I used as a reel for marlin.

I have a picture of us on a snow machine.
Me in a fake leather flight cap,
Grampa dressed in green holding the cardboard tube.
It amplified sound, it bent the world.

The corners of his basement were stacked like a jigsaw,
everything he could not throw away: cardboard sheets,
nails he'd straightened, lumber, faucets, anonymous metal.
After the dry days, he'd never be short again.

And while he dug, long before me,
Grandma in her kitchen made cinnamon rolls
listening for any shift in the ground.

The Ages Of (2)

silica teeth
are windows on the grass blade

studious
as a chimp with a termite stick

skewed parking
after hours in the hospital lot

the clipped steps
from the car to the cathedral

Invasive Technologies: Unsaid and Scattered

to burn up like webbing,
  sparks racing each strand.

                              all this time, we've been missing
                                the moon's bright Eden

    winter cannot pass through

                        you, seed, know the wheel
                        as no machine can know it

because something's always burning,
and someone's always saying
you're crazy to carry that hose.

There are bees in the garden down back

what can be done with the cactus
ravens leave on your doorstep

In the pine circle
where he didn't kiss you
In unruly corners
God forgot to primp
there is magic older than Earth

memories fade,
they must

a movie about creation and death,
creation and death, creation

                    that summer
                    Rodney pulled something ancient
                    from the lake

We live in your imagination

                I remember walking the blank streets at night,
                strobe lights red through your hair.

we are alive in dreams,
live in dreams we cannot imagine,
and this another dream

the grackle's sandal-slap bark
scares the cat

feels like it sounds

light grows and someone
rouses from the dark house

I am nowhere near as interesting
as I thought I'd be by now

Heat and lift
and light moves
the sky.
They do things.
All the time
doing things.
They never stop.
You have to admire
their persistence.

Walking the pilled road,
I dream of other places.
It is orange, the door I've imagined,
with sharp, lazy hinges.
I have been told to expect a garden.

                              Activists burn trees online.

    a long life in segments,
    moments and the puzzlement of movement.
    How does your night live in you?
    she says poems make her sad
    and mean nothing to her

            if my vindictiveness can't cure immortality
            nothing will

He'd been on the hill overlooking the house,
a transistor radio playing Jim Croce
when the car stopped.

Where did the man get that sharp anger?
"It will all come down on you one day,"
and David felt guilt.

Although he had done nothing but watch
the green world below roll in the wind.
It would be a year

before the land was sold, another
year before the trees came down, but still
he'd known all along.

When I have fears
    my soul is lost
    and everything around me
    dream, fiction,
    I light candles
    and rest the world
    against the ear's soft lens.

    I light candles and bow
    in the place that stopped me.

            bound in a love
            that loses form
            with every vessel

I was Irish in the playground
until one of the kids caught on
that the question was fixed

    on the riverside
    near the abandoned hospital
    a helipad, daisies

    red-bellied birds
    catch flies on the slow river
    between cities, the stretch of bright water

    a slab of breakwall
    in the rocks along the shore,
    the throne of the birch gods

            written on a bench
            in a nook in the park:
            "sorry for logging your beach"
            ground-out cigarettes,
            twisted at the charred ends

he stared at the sun and sneezed
I am allergic, said the boy,
to the sun

film of ice on the pond
man on zamboni
mulching leaves

the morning news:
a shooting, a stabbing
a shooting, a stabbing
a story about electric skin

east of the duck pond
the air gets foul

walk to that still point
filled with history and,
empty, walk back

everywhere there are rules
against slumber
and illusions of wakefulness

rules and illusions

a clichéd peace,
late afternoon,
waterfront

I swear there is a loon,
cormorant perhaps,
on the sheath river

the sandstone mansion
near the rapids
with turbines in the basement

student pilot over the park
her English teacher
writes in the blue book

a fire in the shipyard,
dull through grey smoke
the long river between us

The farmer who studies wind and lift
in the field is watching
the spin of wheat,
the current's hand
playing the stalks.

It is how
you are blinking
to the signal light's click
and drumming your thumbs
on the wheel

Believing that gravity keeps the soul in the body,
she avoids astronauts

on blue days
he marvels at the press of the sky,
its million likenesses

bird or barge?
what song in the depth of June?
Birdsong? Bargesong?
The song of echoing despair.

What mind thought
to split the crow's tongue
and wound it
into human speech?
The crow is brought down
to us.

My email program says,
"There are seventy-five unread males."

I am glad for the company

A Distance That Is No Distance

To measure the universe, limbless in its balled-up depth,
cradled at the core, nothing extreme or out of centre, even the
most far-flung molecule, alone on its ride past earth is having a
dance with the nearest star. The subject lets her mind roll out,
knowing there is no distance too remote, no remoteness at all
in fact, just an unseen link, the connection of the thing called
god to the word named god, and that word to the tongue
birthing the word, mother to no misspoken echo: the loss, its
name, the sinking of teeth into skin, desire breeding the dream
that propels the movement of waves, shadows when shadow is
just the body. The subject eats, the subject sleeps. The subject
wants to stand on water.

through distance, a sun becomes a star

our sun a star to someone, to us

She stepped into the projector's beam,
the word mage on her forehead.

                    Fox where the trails meet
                    trades his cell phone
                    for telepathy.

        The crows calling, "Hey.
        One, Two, Three, Hey."

                    The experience is waiting
                    for the bow of the tanker
                    to pass through the branches
                    that block the ship's name.
                    The Brouchlen, eventually it's known.

                    Two geese low over the river, hiccoughing.

We smoked something that looked like curls of cinnamon bark
stacked inside a taco shell. The ash and embers fell.
I gathered up the glowing bits, orange jewels that were eating
through the floorboards, and was surprised they didn't burn my hand.
You told me these are the stones bangers carry to prove they don't give a damn.
I wondered how anyone could keep them from burning
everything and what to line my pockets with should I try
to carry them home.

The Next Poem

i.

There is an echo here.
Without a design, the container
determines the shape.

Copper is at least as valuable
as gold and less vain. Do you
mind if I ask the questions?

Every Sunday crows
on the garden rail
wait for me to finish breakfast.

I have never seen a thunderbird,
but I've seen crows, their eyes
rimmed with starlight
waiting on the garden rail.

I wonder, does a reflection
recognize the body? Does
the container resent the shape
it defines? Again with the questions.

I walked into a wall
after shaking your hand.
You were so beautiful.

I have never dreamed about Facebook.
Therefore, it doesn't exist –
not really.

ii.

Water's slow dance is ice.
Fire's architecture is a doorway.

Highways echo the footpaths
and tradeways we've tried to erase.

Pavement is history's reset
and does the hard work of forgetting.

The winner arranged the furniture
so the best seat has the best view.

Yes, that painting has always been there.
No, we've not changed the wallpaper.

And there never was a mound city
near the downtown Super Mall.

The Overstory

"Happiness Is…"

The rifles were painted green
like leaves and limbs.

You could hang berries
from the barrel and a bear
might walk up thinking
it just another mountain ash
in a typical autumn forest.

The bear would be wrong.
The spark from that limb
would pound ducks from the pond,
and send the bear to its dream den.

He brings them out, all twenty-eight,
so the men in the dining room
can gush at the beauty of concealment,
at that poison under green.

You Can't Expect a Thing Like That

This morning I wrote her name
across a sheet of coarse paper
and tried to remember her face,
the student who left
after planning for September.

There are so many, year after year.
You love them, many of them.
Some, you'd like to forget. Some,
you forget without trying.

In all, you see the babies they were,
the necessary love that leads them
through their first prone days,
through the struggles and entitlements
that bring them to you,

the morning news
that leaves you wishing for time.

Technology Questionnaire

Can you write with a pencil or pen?	Y	N
Do you prefer the keyboard?	Y	N
Have you kept a diary or a blog?	Y	N
Do you write stories, poems, songs?	Y	N
Can you illustrate your writings?	Y	N
Do you see a ghost?	Y	N

For P.B.

The house was mad with men
flexing strange obsessions.
One absorbed with biceps.
Another inhaling vapour
from a foil plate. More singing
junky songs, the clock on midnight.
Television always drawing
tales with a cartoon dog.

I rang the bell, but the bell didn't work,
and so walked into the wild ocean
where she was lacing her boots.
Plastered on one steel toe, a sticker
from the Ministry of Labour showing
a worker lifting a box and below that image
the words: Bend At The Knees.

She said she's been ignored
and kicked space from the room
where the stoner boys, set on pause,
played away their last days.
In the hallway, halfway outside,
halfway into the squalling room,
halfway in the air, I knelt where she'd stood.
Knelt, and prayed to no god I knew
that we might find ourselves
one day where we should be.

Even now, I am waiting for grand circumstance,
for the signal that begins me. Even now,
with little evidence, I believe
fate has favoured us somehow
over every possible version we've left behind.
It is you that my mind assembles,
as I dream you were. And we,
briefly between life's true happening.

The static of those boys, that house, sent me
out. Rising from the hall where I knelt,
I rewound the steps to the sidewalk,
recalled the miles I had walked
to kneel in your absence. It is how I go
and for a moment find my peace.

An Untrue Poem

When you first come in,
sit in a comfortable chair.
Even if someone is sitting there already,
sit beside them.

There is a brown dog on the table.
It is your friend. Speak
to the brown dog. Say,
Hi brown dog. I am your friend.

You can say anything you like,
as long as you speak to the brown dog.

It will not answer. The brown dog
is not a dog. The brown dog is
the cover of a tissue box. If
you need a tissue no one will mind.

Take a tissue from the brown dog.
See how the tissue you take
is replaced by a new tissue
from the back of the brown dog?

That is what happens
when you leave.

War

Or was the sky grieving,
perhaps not at war,
not avenging the drowned boy
but mourning his death?

Weightless

Alive and not knowing,
understanding only
the horror when your grip
gives and you, about to fall,
believing you will walk away,
walk away.

The Sounding Joy

She worries that light
from the first star
will never reach us.

Each morning, the hill
behind the maple
is lashed by tire tracks.

If she wears red shoes, it will rain.
If she forgets to call ahead,
no one will be there when she arrives.

X-Walk

When a student from first-year composition
laughs about driving through a walk light
as her professor crosses the street,
jokes she would have run him down
had he been walking just a bit faster,
had he left the office two seconds earlier,
not stopped to pick up the eraser he'd dropped,
or neglected to marvel
at the play of light in the browning leaves,

it is time, when this happens, to revisit
the function of narrative
on the development of empathy.

The same professor, his shoulders curled,
glasses too big for his face,
tells us the decline of literary enjoyment
and the disappearance of empathy
are linked, but we cannot assume
causality: both facts might be chicken,
might be egg, might be the thing before chicken
that laid the egg.

"The question is," he says, "Does reading
enhance empathy? Is empathy enhanced
by reading?"

He gives no answer,
but assigns a ten-page paper on the subject.

Think of that as you drive home tonight, he says.

Diving for the Stone

I watch the spot where the cormorant went under,
knowing that the river, although slow, has changed
and the spot I've been watching is gone.

On the lamppost a herring gull
Michelangelo could not carve
more beautifully from stone,
yodels for company and spoils the illusion.

A mother duck, with thirteen babies trailing,
brackets down into the cormorant deep.
Her ducklings, diving after, topple like commas
and leave no pause on the surface.

It might be I drowned in my drive for the gold stone.
The girl on the dock tossing the stone over our heads,
far into deep water, and the boys diving under.
The whole lake pounding the ear,
compressing the air in our lungs.

And we'd do this all afternoon,
her brothers and I fighting for the stone.
They are the first to quit.
They know the purpose of the game,
having been born into it.

But I needed the stone, the tickle of her hand
on my fingers as she takes it from me,

and I go down squeezing my lungs out,
shuttering the body's call for survival.
The gold stone grey in the murky light.

This is how far I will go for you,
I say without saying it.
Without even knowing
what's being said,
I say it.

Mayfly

It was later I learned of their blindness.

Sight without eyes. Taste and no mouth.
The filament of the body,
the hooked and translucent thing,
a tail without sting, the wings
like ribbed cellophane.

Calibrated for sex.

What would you do with one day?
Sightless. Without taste.

Hideous like a nightmare,
and driven to mate.

Some have lived a lesser time.
Some not at all.
And here they are,
parked in rows on the door
their wings closed into fins.

We used them as bait,
threaded the hook
through the hollow body
and dropped it twitching for bass.

Although we never caught a thing that way.

A whole day gone
and the fly gone with it.

In the north lakes
we called them shadflies.

Say that anywhere else
and no one will know what you mean.

Mayfly everywhere but north
where they come in June
and later, August, late with the heat
coming late in the north.

The urge at the end of summer.

Stop Motion

They are digging the churchyard.
Men with shovels. Men standing around.
They freeze to watch and call.
One crosses himself, kisses the black cross
that hangs from his neck
when his partners thrust their hips
at the women walking by.

They're digging space for a sewer line.
Before long, the pastor's out there, digging.
The crew is sent away
and the pastor and two friends
take up spades. They dig and glance
to the sky to see if anyone is watching.

It turns out, a time capsule
was the hard blink of blade on wood,
not a casket as the workers thought.
Set into the ground before the church stood,
when a grove and trout stream were landmarks,
ages before concrete, long before Christ
arrived with the sails.

And whether the box was buried as a cornerstone
or if the church just grew from that point
I can't tell from the window.

The pastor kneels on the grass
and plucks the box from the ground,
sliding it out like a sliver.

Everything Was Fine

And after is like waking.
This life seems a permanent condition

until the next now,
the always—
some have said—
now, when the bird
leans away
to clear the hedge,
its shadow on the mirrored lake.

Cicadas, For the Most Part, Are Diurnal

So you have written a poem
for yourself, for no one else,
and you read the poem
to the sky on a clear night,
just the stars and your poem,
you and the breeze in the dark
over the legendary hum of cicadas.

What else? A memory
dog-tailing this memory.

Walking, Seen

a blue jay, the sky in its mouth,
high wire act above the sidewalk,
chattering through the early noise:
vice of cars and the vanity of horns,
the thick sadness of children at the bus stop,
music from the old woman's study—soon,
her typing begins—
the ice edge of autumn these mornings.

Overlooked by Recent Forecasts

It takes a lifetime to remember. And lately
there is a storm inside the building
when the fire alarm sounds and no
fire then winds, rain like we've not seen,
a crow singing its sermon to the cats
and the gulls, with one human nearby
who happened to hear it all.

"Shoe" is the sound
closest to the sound before thunder,
a general shushing in the mind.
A flat sole inching along sand,
the sand on glass or ice,
winter underfoot,
the collective gasping at lightning,
then the stillness before thunder.

Timing

To be that moment
when the ice
breaks and to step
in before the fight begins.

The street is toxic
with the violence of weekends.
Laughter at night
is the weapon.

If I leave the house
at the moment that leads me
into the throw of bodies,
just before the police arrive,
keep hands in my pockets
and elbows blocking kidneys,
hunched, knees ready for the spring,
we might miss the story
that turns us into everyone else,
the prize that will carry
us through the winter.

The Fifth Horseman Rides Again, Briefly

Repenthe, the fifth horsemen, arrives
when the ruins are skinned in green,
when blue begins to ink the sky,
and seasons become recognizable,
when humanity settles into the new
life greed has made. Here, he says, here is pain.
Remember, scourged from the earth,
all that you were. Now this brown,
burning ash, now this lightning bed
and its constant thunder. Now this final
hand no one will forget.

Poem

with the sound down
time's caesium heart,
every clock hand clutching
the pulse, the atom in its housing
counts orbit, counts revolution

at the end of distance,
time and direction stops,
and this happens now
far away from us,
deep in our centres

Cataloguing Solitude

Walking the waterfront,
McCartney in one ear,
the fountain in the other,
a baby says hi
with his palm and fingers out,
the rest of his family distracted
in talk that blinds them to me,
two mergansers hopping up stream,
I realize I'd never seen a male merganser before,
and there he is.

Someone passing by says the universe is being born.
And I ask if it's true, or are we
just learning to recognize its sentience?

The baby in the stroller says hi again
but it's years that have gone, his family
is gone, and he is a policeman one day
and the plumber I call the next.

I will never be alone.

America Before the War: Prophecy

It was said that I would die
an old man on the shore of a great body of water,
die after saving a child from drowning –
one selfless act to hinge a life of self.

So when she calls in the dark from her bed
to the mat by the window she prepared for me,
to ask if I'd rather get a knitting needle in the eye
or die by a razor wound to the groin,
I know someone is wrong.

Either the wolf woman down the street,
dreamcatchers and crystals on the walls
and shelves of her little brick shop,
lied for her five bucks,
or my host in her bed is dreaming.

I lost my fear by staring into starless night.
In that room, dim shapes of the black air around me
begin to take forms not solely from the mind.
In time, the eyes open to the dark.

How To Know

Little should rattle us now.
We've seen rocks
fall to invent the Earth,
and blurred equations
that elude scientific repetition,
microbes that are poison to us,
and a universe made from our thoughts.

Hostages

Trapped in France,
our host gone mad
we watch international ads
that take ages from our lives.

I used to dream about this, I say.
You say, I always knew
you were a bit sick.
I say, I've never dreamed
you before. And that
is how we escape,
the maid along with us,
diving into the van
when the driver stops
to check the tires.

You didn't know I was a hero.
How does that change our lives
where you are never flustered
and I am always frightened?

Tonight

Four moons and Jupiter a star,
the distant swans gargling.
These are ghosts, it was thought.

In the bay, resting before flight,
here like a scent
the wind can't remember.

Flowers Seem To Be How the Universe Measures Gratitude

About Wordsworth and his *spots of time*,
I wanted to say that poems come from moments
that shimmer somehow, when everything shines
through its brevity, and thought:
it's not enough, I need to say more.

Picnic at Carmen's

Thorn people in the dry leaves
understand the overstory,
their myth etching
pendulous to the ground,
becoming the ground itself;
not humus—as if
the components of soil
had walked and dreamed the tree
from the memory of falling.

Midsummer Roadwork

The east-west roads are torn
leaving no access to the north forest
or the water to the south,
and all night airplanes
strobe in blue perforations.

The city is over. There, is death
from starvation. Here, is death
from abundance. Everywhere,
even in Arcadia, the old bard says.

Tonight the last exit is withdrawn.
It takes a year to get out, around the pylons
and sawhorse barricades that corral the pit.

Some flawless and invented hell
in the strand between cities
swallows the traveler, the escape artist, the hero.

Stand clear, the sign would say,
if anyone had bothered to post a sign
and if signs could speak.

Wendell, I Hope We Got Lucky

We dance before we know the steps,
confident that we are guided. By what,
I don't know. Memory? A map
made by shadowy gods?

Wendell, I was misery to you.

Awake

At 5 a.m. with nowhere to go;
where to go at 5 a.m.?
Looking for poems
and finding a few—
etchings on onion skin
laid against dry stone,
clouds made from charcoal,
that sort of thing.

The twelfth grader knows more
about Freud and Aristotle
than I ever knew,
but I no longer try to seem wise.
Instead, I say, "Is that so?"
With genuine surprise,
"Is that so?"

All in a junk boat of voices,
distinct like threads in a weave.
The colour of joy.

Notes and Acknowledgements

I would like to thank the Ontario Arts Council for its generous support during the writing and revision process. A belated thank you to Professor Jim Gibson, whose courses in Canadian poetry and thought were an inspiring and formative experience. Thanks, too, to John Buschek and BuschekBooks for putting it out there.

Contact: www.mddunn.com

Versions of the following poems have been previously published:

"Crimes," *Contemporary Verse 2*
"January Thaw," *Great Lakes Review*
"Sustaining Wonder," *Fat City Review*

Other Titles by M. D, Dunn

Ghost Music (2010)
Fancy Clapping (2012)